dirty
little secrets

from

OTHERWISE PERFECT MOMS

dirty
little secrets

from

OTHERWISE PERFECT MOMS

TRISHA ASHWORTH *and* AMY NOBILE

CHRONICLE BOOKS

SAN FRANCISCO

Library of Congress Cataloging-in-Publication Data available.

ISBN: 978-0-8118-6390-2

Manufactured in Canada

Design by Jennifer Tolo Pierce

10 9 8 7 6 5 4 3

Chronicle Books LLC
680 Second Street
San Francisco, California 94107

www.chroniclebooks.com

A huge and heartfelt thank you to our editor Lisa Campbell.

to all moms

*who are courageous enough to speak the truth, lift the veil,
and tell it like it really is. Your honesty puts us one step closer
to loving motherhood as much as we love our kids.*

Introduction

Reluctant as many of us may be to admit it, we moms have all got dirty little secrets. Whether we've got one child or five, a 50-hour-a-week job or full-time duty as supermom, we've all got a few small, not-for-public-discussion, yet utterly crucial coping mechanisms. A couple stealthy habits or indulgences we rely on in times of need, and then conveniently neglect to tell our partners or closest friends.

We, the authors, also have more than a few dirty little secrets of our own. What's more, after interviewing more than a hundred moms to write our first book, *I Was a Really Good Mom Before I Had Kids,* we discovered that pretty much every mother out there does as well. Of course, no one wants to admit that, at least at first. But once we got moms talking, anonymously, and once we'd listened to their initial raps about how truly *amazing* and *balanced* and *blessed* their whole lives are, we burrowed down to the truth.

This process of emotional realization took a few minutes. Twenty-two to be exact.

Us: How are you handling motherhood right now?
Them: It's amazing. I love it! I am so balanced. My husband is my best friend. . . .

Twenty-two minutes later:
Us: Sounds like you have a real balance in your life. How do you do it?
Them: Ummmm, well, maybe balance isn't the right word. Ummm, actually, I haven't taken a shower in three days. And, OK, my husband and I haven't had sex in three weeks. . . .

Then, after the truth about sex and hygiene, came the secrets—the late-night grocery-store runs to buy milk, just to steal a few minutes alone; or the phony "latte names" used at Starbucks and the elaborate fantasy lives that went along with those names, primarily involving still living in the city and not having kids. When we first stumbled upon these secrets, we added a few of them to our book, on the theory that even a mom with a howling newborn and a terrorist *"don't-make-me-hurl-this-mac-and-cheese-at-you"* toddler could home in and hit pay dirt in the five seconds a day she managed to read. We thought of the secrets as mom candy: a quick, delicious hit. What we didn't yet see—in fact, what we didn't realize until moms from near and far started telling us—is that those secrets aren't just juicy. They tell a whole story. Packed into mom shorthand, each contains a highly condensed accounting of the issues we're all living with in motherhood today.

So we went on a mission to uncover more. In some cases moms mailed us their typewritten dirty little secrets to ensure their privacy—they wouldn't risk being identified by their handwriting or sharing their e-mail address. In others, moms approached us in person, eager to share their own realities, both for the sake of connecting and for the catharsis of coming clean. We hope you'll read the secrets that follow in the spirit that we gathered them: without endorsement, without judgment, but in solidarity. Our goal is to puncture the overblown expectations we all have of ourselves to be "perfect," and in the process make our generation of mothers feel less guilty, less burdened, more unified, and less alone.

Talk to us and other moms at
www.reallygoodmom.com.

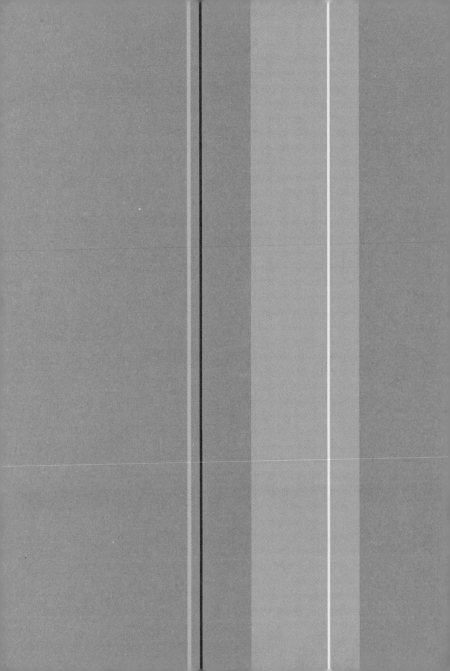

chapter one

DIRTY LITTLE SECRETS

My secret escape is *having a cigarette with my husband* in the back of my minivan while the kids are inside watching a movie.

My kids don't wear pj's on weeknights. They *go to bed in their school clothes* so I don't have to fight with them about their outfits in the morning.

I let my two toddlers eat Milk Bones right out of the box. I figure *if they're not barking,* they're fine.

I signed my son up for karate because

the instructor is hot.

I lie to my mother in-law **so it seems like I spend more time with the kids than I do.**

My biggest fear as a mother
is being judged by other moms.

I had to use *my toddler's potty chair*
on the side of the road when I was stuck
in traffic. I just couldn't hold it.

I love my kids *but I didn't always.*

It took time to fall in love with them.

I wish my husband
would have gotten
hair plugs

before it was

too late.

The hardest part about being a
working mom is the "mom" part.

If I repeat to myself *"I'm OK, I'm OK,"*
I hope that I'll begin to believe it.

My one regret in motherhood is

_____

that I can't
slap people.

I skip *whole chunks* of my younger daughter's bedtime stories. Poor thing really can't tell the difference.

I threw away my birth control pills
and *he doesn't know.*

Sometimes I think my nanny does *a better job* than I do.

Last night I wanted to read my book

so I let my three- and five-year-olds

watch reruns of *Roseanne.*

My shrink tells me we have to laugh more.

What a *waste of money.*

My night nurse was my crack addiction.

She was supposed to stay for two weeks.

She stayed for six months.

I threw out a pair of shoes my daughter loved
and told her *I couldn't find them.*

I told my four-year-old daughter *that it's illegal* to get married before you're twenty-nine.

When I'm at Safeway I buy a
Nordstrom gift card and charge it as groceries.
I can justify it that way.

My rule is beer at lunch, wine at 5.
Wine at lunch feels like I have a "problem"
but beer just seems OK.

I locked my two-year-old daughter in my car and stood helplessly as I watched her take her hair clip out of her hair and put it *in her mouth.*

I bit my daughter's finger
while trying to steal a bite out
of her cookie.

Some nights when my husband
and I go to bed, *I roll over and "play dead."*
All I can think is "I just can't handle it if
one more person pokes me today."

I lie about my babysitting hours
to my friends—"oh, I have her eight hours,"
when in reality it's twenty.

chapter two

DIRTIER LITTLE SECRETS

I missed my child's *first day* of kindergarten.

Sometimes *I feel guilty*

for liking going to work so much.

My seven-year-old-son *walked in on us* having sex. We told him we were doing karate in bed.

We were in the grocery store

and when we hit the wine aisle, she screamed,

"That's Mommy's juice!"

Note to husband: **Dinner?**
Don't even ask. There is no dinner. There will
never be dinner. Just stop coming home hungry.
Unless you have a plan, there will be no plan.
And by the way,

I'm hungry, too.

Once I realized my husband
was *not my girlfriend*, it made my life
so much easier.

get annoyed at my kids for picking their noses.

But I do it too.

I lied and told my son's preschool
that he was potty trained so he could get in.
I acted surprised when he had an
"accident" every day.

After our family vacation,
I secretly checked myself into the spa
for the day.

I never ask for help. I don't kn
I feel like asking for help wo
I have failed in some

My husband thinks I'm sad when he
goes on business trips, *but secretly, I'm happy*
that my "third child" is out of the house.

I know the exact day

my son was conceived because it was the *only* day

we had sex that month.

Planning dinner usually throws me over the edge. One night I was stressing out and my four-year-old son looked up at me and said *"Just order a f*$%in' pizza!"*

When I'm hosting a dinner party,

I buy premade food and pass it off as my own.

I wrap everything in tin foil to make it look legit,

turn on the stove to heat up the kitchen and make

just enough of a mess. I make sure to dispose of

the "evidence" (containers) beforehand. Even

my husband has no clue.

My strict "no toy gun" policy eventually
relaxed into a "if you make it yourself" policy,
and then finally into a *"if you shoot at
someone, aim at their feet"* policy.

I had kids because

My husband makes a lot less money
than I do and sometimes that's just *not sexy.*

I routinely fake having a cold or cough
so I can escape to the guest room and
have the bed all to myself. And the bonus is,
I'm "sick"—so if one of the kids gets up,
it's my husband's problem.

My kids yell because I yell at them.

One morning I was rushing out the door to a business meeting and I couldn't find my travel mug. So I poured my coffee into *my son's sippy cup* and drank it in my car on the way to work.

I hate the way my husband chews.
I can hear it from a mile away.

I do my son's homework just so we can *get through it faster.* I grab his pencil and he just looks at me like I've lost my mind.

I never thought I'd send my daughter
to daycare, so I *just call it preschool* and
it makes me feel better.

My husband and I have a *secret trade-off.*
The more dishes he unloads and laundry he folds the
higher the chance he'll "get some" that night.

I had to *lock myself in my car* to make
a conference call while my kids screamed and
banged on the window outside.

I fear being alone with
all three of my kids for any
extended period of time.

Like an hour or more.

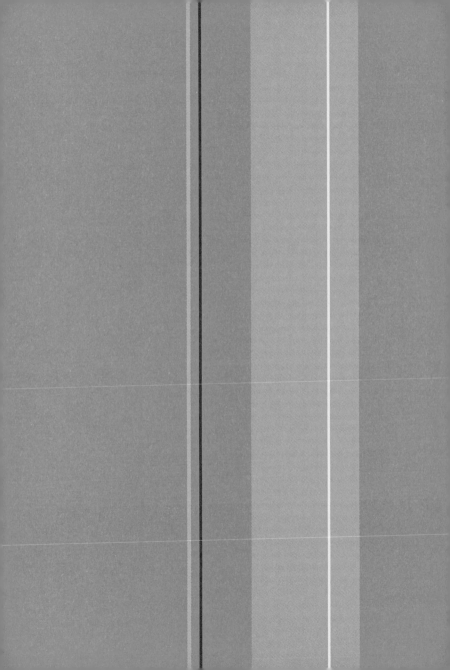

chapter three

EVEN DIRTIER LITTLE SECRETS

I look at every mother and I assume that they're a *much better mother* than I am.

I never, ever hire *a good-looking babysitter.*

Why put candy in front of a baby?

Being a "single" mom

is the world's best-kept secret.

My son threw a colossal tantrum in the middle
of a nice boutique. To stop the screaming
I took the gum out of my mouth and shoved
it into his. Then I realized that all five people
in the store including the manager were
looking at me *completely horrified.*

I take *VICODIN* when the baby won't stop crying.

I just got *passed over* for a promotion

and I was secretly like "Yay!"

I pass gas and *blame it on the kids.*

Once I realized my neighbors
could hear me over the baby monitor
(we were on the same frequency), I suddenly
changed my tone and became
"sweet, nice Mommy."

We forgot to buckle our two-year-old up in the car . . .
when we went around the corner, he flew over
to the next seat and screamed "f*#$ers!!"

Sometimes I *purposely stay at work* one hour longer at the end of the day so I "miss" the bedtime routine.

The one thing I wish

I had *is a wife.*

I take like four showers a day.

Because showers are allowed.

I forgot to pick my boy up
from kindergarten because *I was too involved*
in a VH1 Rockumentary.

I'm mortified that my three-year-old daughter keeps going up to complete strangers and asking, *"Do you want to see my penis?"*

My husband would be really surprised

if he knew that I think he's *the most amazing person*

I've ever met. I'm just too busy to tell him.

I sat and *spied on my hot handyman* **drilling holes in my walls.**

When I see a newborn, *I want to puke.*

My daughter busted me *using my Blackberry* during one of her school plays.

I want to *smack the mom* who says "You only have one child?"

I've never admitted this to anyone else
but I have *pinched my daughter's arms* so hard
I leave a mark.

My kids beg me to get in the pool with them.

I tell them I can't swim.

It would *ruin my highlights.*

I prayed to have kids because it took

so long to get pregnant, but even now, when they're

eight and ten, I'm sad to admit that being a stay

at home mom doesn't complete me.

My husband would be really surprised if he knew that I *thought about divorce* more times than I can count.

I send my kids to camp and *charge it to my secret credit card* so my husband never knows how expensive it really is.

It's *impossible to keep my house clean* so I just don't invite people over. Ever.

I have *sex with myself*

more than with
my husband.

Thank God a hidden camera didn't catch me . . .

changing my tampon in my car.

I tell my husband I am going to go potty but actually *lock myself in the bathroom,* sit on the edge of the tub, and read *People.*

After having kids I've finally realized
that the really big moments in life are actually
the small ones. And those moments
make it all worth it.